Workplace Harassment Awareness and Prevention

Workplace harassment defined
The business case for workplace harassment prevention
Proven strategies to prevent workplace harassment
2016 Select Task Force Report
Bystander intervention training

© 2018 HRComplianceTraining.Net. All rights reserved.

Except as permitted under the U.S. Copyright Act of 1976, no part of this publication may be reproduced, distributed, or transmitted in any form or by any means, or stored in a database or retrieval system, without the prior written permission of the publisher.

Publisher: HRComplianceTraining.Net
180 North University Avenue – Suite 270 - Provo, UT 84601

Author: Davy Z. Jones
First Edition: November 2018

ISBN: 9781731234520

The author and publisher have made every effort to ensure that the information in this publication was correct at the time of publication. The author and publisher do not assume and hereby disclaim any liability to any party for any loss, damage, or disruption caused by errors or omissions, whether such errors or omissions result from negligence, accident, or any other cause.

DISCLAIMERS – This publication was produced to provide general knowledge about workplace harassment awareness and prevention. Information presented herein is intended to be used for general educational purposes only and should not be construed to be offered in any way as legal advice, counsel, or opinion(s).

NO LEGAL ADVICE OFFERED - Content herein is not intended to convey or constitute legal advice, is not intended to be a solicitation of any kind, and is in no way is a substitution for legal advice obtained from a qualified attorney. We advise you to consult with a qualified employment law attorney for answers to questions relative to your particular situation.

USE OF THIS PUBLICATION - This publication is licensed for your personal use only and may not be re-sold or given away. If you would like to share this publication with colleagues, family, friends, or students, please purchase an additional copy for each person (quantity discounts are available; contact us at info@hrcompliancetraining.net for details).

Written and produced in the United States of America.

Workplace Harassment Awareness and Prevention

Book Contents

Workplace harassment defined 7

The business case for workplace harassment awareness and prevention 9

Proven strategies to maintain awareness of and prevent workplace harassment 12

2016 Select Task Force Report on the Study of Harassment in the Workplace 15

Summary 25

Resources 28

This book is dedicated to the hard working women and men who deserve to be treated with dignity and respect as they make the economy go and grow.

Workplace Harassment Awareness and Prevention　　DavyZJones

"Am I not destroying my enemies when I make friends of them?" ~ Abraham Lincoln

Workplace Harassment Awareness and Prevention   DavyZJones

Workplace Harassment

Awareness and Prevention

Workplace harassment defined

Workplace harassment is defined by the U.S. Equal Employment Opportunity Commission (EEOC) as offensive or unwelcome conduct in any form perpetrated on a co-worker by a colleague, a supervisor, an employer's agent or even a non-employee.

Harassment is an action or attitude against another person because of his or her age, ancestry, arrest record, citizenship status, color, gender, genetics, marital status, military status, physical, mental or perceived disability or handicap, national origin, race, religion, or sexual orientation (including gender identity).

Workplace harassment interferes with the victim's ability to perform his or her job or to advance professionally or is harmful to that person's mental well-being.

Harassment in action includes but is not limited to epithets, insults, intimidation, mockery, name-calling, offensive jokes, physical assaults, physical threats, presentation of offensive objects or pictures, put-downs, ridicule, slurs, unwanted attention, or unwelcome contact in any form. Harassment becomes illegal whenever an employee must endure the offensive behavior to remain employed or when a reasonable person would consider the action to be abusive, hostile, intimidating or inappropriate. Simple interpersonal annoyances, petty slights, and minor, isolated conflicts are not found to be illegal acts of harassment.

The business case for workplace harassment awareness and prevention

Harassment in any form in the workplace hurts your most valuable asset – *the women and men who make everything happen* – and is therefore ethically and morally wrong on every level, a fact which makes every employer ethically and morally responsible for making every effort to be aware of and prevent any form of workplace harassment.

Moreover, workplace harassment kills profitability. According to the U.S. Equal Employment Opportunity Commission (EEOC), employers lost $164.5 million in 2015 in potential profits paid to employees who were victims of workplace harassment. These losses were in addition to the hundreds of millions of dollars in lost profits paid to harassed employees who prosecuted their cases, without EEOC intervention, in local, state, and federal courts.

Preventing workplace harassment
makes economic sense for two reasons:

1. **Direct costs** – includes costs for energy, resources, and time diverted from business operations to confront and assess an act of workplace harassment, hire legal

representation, appear for depositions, appear in court, and for court-awarded damages, fines, judgments, and settlements. Between 2010 and 2015, employers paid nearly $700 million in compensation to harassed employees through the EEOC's pre-litigation process. These direct costs are in addition to hundreds of millions of dollars in post-trial awards ordered to be paid by judges and juries plus countless millions of dollars employer/defendants spent on court costs and lost employee time.

2. **Indirect costs** – includes countless millions of dollars in lost productivity, increased employee turnover, and damage to an organization's brand and reputation. Even the mere allegation of workplace harassment can interfere with an organization's ability to attract new employees and to retain customers or clients or to attract new customers or clients. When any employee is victimized by harassment, productivity is likely to suffer because harassed employees are often driven to disengage from job responsibilities, become distracted, neglect projects, begin to show up late to work or may even stop showing up at all. Workplace harassment

stresses not only employees who are direct targets but also puts stress on employees who may witness acts of harassment or may be aware of harassing behavior. When employers begin to calculate the costs of workplace harassment, they see how minutes, hours, days, weeks, and months of productivity lost to the ramifications of workplace harassment can become a severe drag on cash flow and profits.

The bottom line is the bottom line . . . every employer understands how costly workplace harassment can be. In Addition to making an employer liable for attorney's fees and court costs and court-ordered damage awards, bullying is harmful to employee morale, destroys productivity, makes it more difficult to retain qualified employees, and can do grim damage to an organization's reputation.

Proven strategies to maintain awareness of and prevent workplace harassment

Senior management commitment - Effectively eliminating the threat of harassment in the workplace is possible only when business owners and senior managers are intractably committed to investing in, promoting, and maintaining a diverse, inclusive, and respectful workplace in which any form of discrimination or harassment is just not tolerated.

Equal, proportionate, discipline for all harassers - The commitment on behalf of owners and senior managers notwithstanding, any organization that hopes to eliminate workplace harassment must be willing to hold any employee accountable, appropriately and meaningfully, for any incidents of harassment. If at any time, an employer discovers a harassing event, discipline should be immediate and proportioned to the severity of the act and should be applied equally to all employees.ac

Implement viable 'zero tolerance' anti-harassment policies and procedures - While leadership and accountability establish the foundation for an employer's anti-harassment culture, viable 'zero tolerance' policies and procedures build the framework to protect employees, clients, and vendors from the threat of workplace harassment.

Survey employees - A first step in communicating the organization's commitment to a harassment-free workplace is to survey employees to determine whether harassment currently exists and to at the same time measure the potential for future incidents. The results of the survey should then be shared with all employees and an open discussion of policies and procedures to remedy any existing or potential problems should ensue.

Develop viable anti-harassment policies and procedures - The next step would be to craft sensible, appropriate anti-harassment policies and procedures, supplemented by objective, relevant training to ensure that all employees understand how to utilize those policies and procedures so they can be constantly aware of, prevent, and accurately report workplace harassment incidents. It is critical to establish a reporting system by which employees who've experienced harassment and employees who observe any potentially harmful behavior can accurately report to designated managers. Anti-harassment policies should include ironclad guarantees against retaliation in any form. For this step to fully succeed, senior management must be willing to give key personnel the authority and power to take appropriate actions to ensure company-wide compliance with anti-harassment policies and procedures.

Invest in objective employment law training - Last but not least, the organization's leadership must be willing to invest the money and time necessary to procure easily accessible, timely harassment awareness and prevention training for employees, key personnel, and senior managers.

2016 Select Task Force Report on the Study of Harassment in the Workplace

A 2016 report issued by the *Select Task Force on the Study of Harassment in the Workplace* says, "We believe effective training can reduce workplace harassment, and recognize that ineffective training can be unhelpful or even counterproductive. However, even effective training cannot occur in a vacuum - it must be part of a holistic culture of non-harassment that starts at the top. Similarly, one size does *not* fit all: Training is most effective when tailored to the specific workforce and workplace, and to different potentially problematic employees. Finally, when trained correctly, middle-managers and first-line supervisors, in particular, can be a valuable resource in helping an employer prevent harassing behaviors."

The Select Task Force study goes on to say, "New and Different Approaches to Training Should Be Explored. We heard of several new models of training that may show promise for harassment training. 'Bystander intervention training' - increasingly used to combat sexual violence on school campuses - empowers co-workers by providing tools to intervene whenever they encounter a harassing behavior and may even work to prevent future incidents of workplace harassment."

The study concludes, "Harassment in the workplace will not stop on its own - it's on all of us to be part of the fight to stop workplace harassment. We cannot be complacent bystanders and expect our workplace cultures to change themselves. For this reason, we suggest exploring the launch of an *It's on Us* campaign for the workplace. Originally developed to reduce sexual violence in educational settings, the *It's on Us* campaign is premised on the idea that students, faculty, and campus staff should be empowered to be part of the solution to sexual assault, and should be provided the tools and resources to prevent sexual assault as engaged bystanders. Launching a similar *It's on Us* campaign in workplaces across the nation - large and small, urban and rural - is an audacious goal. But doing so could transform the problem of workplace harassment from being about targets, harassers, and legal compliance, into one in which co-workers, supervisors, clients, and customers all have roles to play in stopping such harassment."

Bystander intervention training

In the fall of 2009, nearly a dozen bystanders stood by and watched as a teenage girl was assaulted outside a California high school. While many of the bystanders had cell phones and some even recorded the attack, no one intervened to stop the assault. Experts define this type of tragedy as 'bystander inaction.'

Bystander inaction results from a phenomenon known as 'bystander effect,' a condition caused by the fact that bystanders are less likely to take action to intervene when they are part of a group.

Bystander intervention training teaches employees why, when, and how to take responsibility for ensuring the safety of their colleagues in the workplace by intervening whenever they witness any form of harassment. This training is designed to change passive bystanders into active bystanders who are capable of effectively discouraging, preventing, and interrupting acts of bullying.

Bystander intervention helps eradicate workplace harassment by:

1. Changing the workforce's perception of what is and what is not acceptable behavior
2. Eliminating a harasser's ability to blame his or her victim
3. Making workplace harassment a community problem requiring a community solution
4. Turning bystanders into allies who can use peer pressure to protect workplace harassment victims

Bystander intervention works when every employee:

1. Is always aware of the potential for workplace harassment and is willing to intervene when necessary
2. Recognizes when an act of bullying is occurring
3. Can determine whether or not to intervene to prevent a potential act of harassment or to stop an in-process act of harassment
4. Is capable of deciding how best to intervene appropriately, safely, and successfully
5. Can safely intervene and successfully diffuse a harasser's action

Who is a bystander?

You are a bystander when you witness a harassing incident but are not directly involved. As a bystander, you have a choice to make: you can do nothing, or you can calmly and safely intervene by discouraging, interrupting, or preventing an incident or you can ask a manager or supervisor to intercede.

Bystander intervention training

Workplace harassment is a growing nationwide epidemic that threatens the economic and social stability of millions of employers of all sizes in all industries.

The U.S. Equal Employment Opportunity Commission (EEOC) reports that it received an average of 76 harassment charges every day in 2015, costing employers nearly $165 million in federal court-ordered awards and settlements.

EEOC statistics do not include estimated hundreds of millions of dollars in legal fees, court costs, or court-awarded awards and settlements associated with harassment actions adjudicated in local and state courts.

Perhaps more importantly, legal costs and court-ordered

awards and settlements are in addition to as much as 359 billion dollars in annual losses* in productivity and employee turnover costs.

How workplace harassment looks like to a bystander

Harassers can hassle others in a variety of ways, including but not limited to:

- Blocking a person's ability to move from one spot to another
- Displaying or sending offensive or suggestive Emails, images, voicemails, or websites
- Making derogatory, offensive, or stereotypical remarks about a person's age, disability, ethnicity, gender, national origin, race, religion, or sexuality
- Making offensive or suggestive gestures
- Staring at another person with a hostile or sexually suggestive expression
- Indecent, unwanted physical contact
- Telling demeaning or suggestive jokes or stories
- Any other behavior that disrupts or threatens the sense of safety and security of any individual or individuals in the workplace

How you can avoid becoming a harasser

While we don't have space here to include every possible scenario, we ask that you ask the following questions about any behavior that might be considered to be harassment. If you are ever tempted to harass anyone in the workplace, you should ask if you would do or make a harassing threat . . .

- In front of your parents, partner, or spouse?
- To your minister, priest, or rabbi?
- To a person of your ethnicity, gender, race, or religion?

Or you might wonder . . .

- Would I want to be on the wrong end of my harassing words or acts?
- Would I harass my family or friends with my inappropriate actions or words?

Okay . . . we've defined the problem . . . so; we'll tell you that the solution is to change the culture in your workplace to make harassment completely unacceptable by embracing 'Bystander Intervention' whenever and wherever possible.

When is bystander intervention appropriate?

Bystander intervention is appropriate when you have the knowledge and skills necessary to safely and effectively help stop an act of harassment.

Let's say that you're at your desk or workstation doing what you do so well when you hear or see person **A** physically, verbally, or sexually harassing person **B**.

What could you do what would you do?

Would you ignore the harassment or would you attempt to put an end to harassing behavior?

While you might want to slug the harasser in the mouth, that would be your worst possible choice for a couple of obvious reasons: 1. Your act of violence could result in the harasser retaliating by physically attacking you and the victim or, 2. You could put yourself in a position of being arrested and prosecuted for felony assault.

A more effective response might be for you to speak up for the victim by making eye contact with the harasser and saying something like:

- "I'm going to call for a supervisor."

- "Knock it off . . . I don't want to call for a supervisor but I will."
- "Please stop . . . we're not here to harass each other; we're here to work."
- "We don't tolerate any form of harassment here."

Or, you might enlist the help of others by:

- Asking a colleague to intervene
- Taking advantage of strength in numbers by convincing a colleague to join you in approaching the harasser to ask him or her to stop

Or, you could express your disdain in a nonverbal way by:

- Frowning or shaking your head
- Walking away to find a supervisor

Call 911 if you ever have a concern about anyone's physical safety

The bottom line

Your willingness to intervene as an innocent bystander will help others to understand that harassment is not acceptable in your workplace and that understanding could be the most powerful tool you'll ever use to help eliminate harassment in your workplace . . . once and for all.

Summary

The ever-changing economy, including the recovery from the 2008 crash and coping with political uncertainties coupled with globalization, has put America's employers and employees under incredible economic pressure. The lack of confidence that accompanies this transformation has, for a variety of reasons, led to significant increases in claims of workplace harassment.

While each harassment claim represents a threat to workplace harmony, productivity, and, ultimately, profitability, an employer can take sensible steps to not only minimize those threats but can also use anti-harassment policies and procedures to help create and sustain a harmonious, productive, profitable workforce.

The following guidelines can help prevent workplace harassment claims and reduce the corresponding drain on profits:

1. **Top-down commitment to eliminate workplace harassment** – Owners, senior managers, and key personnel must publicly make personal commitments

to promoting civility and respect along with zero tolerance policies and procedures against workplace harassment, thereby discouraging employees from engaging in harassing conduct.

2. **A transparent, concise, confidential reporting process** – The process should guarantee that any employee who is a victim of workplace harassment or is aware of workplace harassment will not have to fear retaliation by colleagues, supervisors, or any other person. If an employer implemented an independent third-party hotline that employees could use to report incidents of workplace harassment, they would be more confident in the employer's commitment to eliminate all forms of workplace harassment.

3. **No retaliation** – An employer's anti-harassment policy should guarantee that management will handle every report of workplace harassment with complete confidentiality and that the employer will protect any person who reports any form of harassment from retaliation.

4. **Anti-harassment training** – An essential part of a viable anti-harassment program is regularly scheduled

training for managers, key personnel, and all other employees. Training can be conducted by trained human resources professionals or employment law attorneys who are willing to meet before any scheduled training sessions to ensure that training meets the specific needs of each employer.

Resources

Christine Porath et al., *It's Unfair: Why Customers Who Merely Observe an Uncivil Employee Abandon the Company*, J. Serv. Res. 1 (2011); Christine Porath et al., *Witnessing Incivility Among Employees: Effects on Consumer Anger and Negative Inferences about Companies*, 37 J. Consumer Res. 292 (2010). The studies generally define "incivility" as insensitive, disrespectful, or rude behaviors directed at another person that displays a lack of regard.

Dawn Nelson, AARP, *AARP Bulletin Poll on Workers 50+: Executive Summary*, Am. Ass'n Retired Persons (2007), *available at* http://assets.aarp.org/rgcenter/econ/workers_poll_1.pdf.

Emily A. Leskinen et al., *Gender harassment: Broadening Our Understanding of Sex-Based Harassment at Work*, 35 Law and Human Behavior 25 (2011) (stating that the Sexual Experiences Questionnaire (SEQ), developed by Professor Louise Fitzgerald and her colleagues in 1988, is the most validated and widely used measure of sexual harassment experiences). *See also* Louise F. Fitzgerald et al., *Measuring Sexual Harassment in the Military: The Sexual Experiences Questionnaire (SEQ-DoD)*, 11 Mil. Psychol. 243 (1998).

Jennifer Vanderminden & Carol Swiech, *Report on the Status of People with Disabilities: A Survey of Faculty and Staff at the University of New Hampshire*, Fall2011.

K.S. Douglas Low et al., *The Experience of Bystanders of Workplace Ethnic Harassment*, 37 J. Applied Social Psychol. 2261 (2007).

Kimberly T. Schneider et al., *An Examination of the Nature and Correlates of Ethnic Harassment Experiences in Multiple Contexts*, 85 J. Applied Psychol. 3 (2000). This study is based on four convenience samples of predominantly Hispanic men and women.

Rodney Peter Gapp & Bill Merrilees, *Important Factors to Consider When Using Internal Branding as a Management Strategy: A Healthcare Case Study*, 14 J. Brand Mgmt. 162 (2006).

Tamara A. Bruce, *Racial and Ethnic Harassment in the Workplace in* Gender, Race, and Ethnicity in the Workplace: Issues and Challenges for Today's Organizations (Margaret Foegen Karsten, ed., 2006). While Title VII prohibits discrimination based on national origin, the research generally looks at harassment based on ethnicity, rather than national origin.

U.S. Equal Employment Opportunity Commission, *Enforcement & Litigation Statistics, All Charges Alleging Harassment* (FY 2010-FY 2015), https://www.eeoc.gov/eeoc/statistics/enforcement/all_harassment.cfm; U.S. Equal Employment Opportunity Commission, *Annual Reports on the Federal Work Force (Part I), EEO Complaint Processing, Fiscal Years 2010-2015*, https://www.eeoc.gov/federal/reports/.

www.ingramcontent.com/pod-product-compliance
Lightning Source LLC
Chambersburg PA
CBHW070945220526
45469CB00007B/2528